Welcome to the exciting world of affiliate marketing! Whether you're a seasoned marketer looking to expand your revenue streams or a newcomer eager to explore the possibilities of online entrepreneurship, this book is your comprehensive guide to mastering the art and science of affiliate marketing.

Affiliate marketing has emerged as one of the most accessible and profitable ways to monetize your online presence, driving sales, and earning passive income by promoting products and services from other companies. With low barriers to entry and limitless potential for growth, affiliate marketing offers individuals and businesses the opportunity to harness the power of the internet to generate revenue and build successful online businesses.

In this book, we'll explore everything you need to know to succeed in affiliate marketing, from the fundamentals of getting started and selecting profitable niches to advanced strategies for driving traffic, optimizing conversions, and maximizing your affiliate revenue. You'll learn how to choose the right affiliate programs, create compelling content, leverage affiliate networks, and navigate legal and ethical considerations to ensure long-term success.

Whether you're interested in affiliate marketing as a side hustle, a full-time business, or simply a way to supplement your income, this book will provide you with the knowledge, tools, and resources you need to thrive in the competitive world of affiliate marketing. Get ready to embark on an exciting journey of discovery, learning, and earning potential as we dive into the world of affiliate marketing together.

Table of Contents

1. Introduction to Affiliate Marketing

2. Understanding Affiliate Networks

3. Choosing Profitable Niches

4. Selecting High-Converting Products

5. Building Your Affiliate Website

6. Crafting Compelling Content

7. Effective Promotion Strategies

8. Email Marketing for Affiliates

9. Harnessing the Power of Social Media

10. Search Engine Optimization (SEO) for Affiliates

11. Paid Advertising Tactics

12. Tracking and Analyzing Performance

13. Optimizing Conversion Rates

14. Scaling Your Affiliate Business

15. Monetization Beyond Affiliate Marketing

16. Legal and Ethical Considerations

17. Overcoming Common Challenges

18. Future Trends in Affiliate Marketing

19. Success Stories and Case Studies

20. Conclusion and Next Steps

21. Resources and Tools

22. Glossary of Affiliate Marketing Terms

23. Index

Each chapter provides concise yet comprehensive information, along with actionable tips and examples to help readers implement strategies effectively. The book aims to cover all essential aspects of affiliate marketing, empowering readers to start and grow their affiliate businesses successfully.

1. INTRODUCTION TO AFFILIATED MARKETING

Welcome to the exciting world of affiliate marketing! In this introduction, we'll explore what affiliate marketing is, why it's such a powerful business model, and how you can leverage it to generate passive income and build a successful online business.

Affiliate marketing is a performance-based marketing strategy where businesses reward affiliates for driving traffic or sales to their website through the affiliate's marketing efforts. As an affiliate marketer, you act as a middleman between the product or service provider and the consumer, earning a commission for each sale or action generated through your promotional efforts.

The beauty of affiliate marketing lies in its simplicity and scalability. Unlike traditional business models that require significant upfront investment and ongoing maintenance, affiliate marketing allows you to start with minimal resources and grow your business at your own pace. Whether you're a seasoned marketer or a complete beginner, affiliate marketing offers endless opportunities for earning passive income and achieving financial freedom.

In the following chapters, we'll dive deeper into the various aspects of affiliate marketing, from choosing profitable niches and products to implementing effective promotional strategies and optimizing your conversion rates. By the end of this book, you'll have the knowledge and tools you need to launch and grow a successful affiliate marketing business, regardless of your background or experience level.

Get ready to embark on an exciting journey of discovery and entrepreneurship. Whether you're looking to supplement your existing income, escape the 9-5 grind, or build a thriving online business, affiliate marketing can help you achieve your goals. So let's dive in and unlock the potential of Affiliated marketing together.

2.UNDERSTANDING AFFILIATED NETWORKS

Affiliate networks serve as intermediaries between affiliates (publishers) and merchants (advertisers) in the affiliate marketing ecosystem. These networks play a crucial role in facilitating partnerships, tracking sales and commissions, and providing valuable resources and support to both affiliates and merchants.

At its core, an affiliate network acts as a platform where merchants can list their products or services for promotion by affiliates. For affiliates, joining an affiliate network provides access to a wide range of products and services to promote, often spanning multiple industries and niches. This diversity allows affiliates to choose products that align with their interests, expertise, and target audience, maximizing their earning potential.

One of the key functions of affiliate networks is tracking affiliate sales and commissions. When an affiliate promotes a merchant's product and generates a sale or action (such as a sign-up or download), the affiliate network tracks this activity using unique tracking links or codes. This ensures that affiliates are credited with the sales they generate, and merchants can accurately calculate and pay commissions.

Affiliate networks also offer various tools and resources to help affiliates succeed. These may include reporting and analytics dashboards to track performance, promotional materials such as banners and creatives, and educational resources and training programs to enhance affiliates' marketing skills.

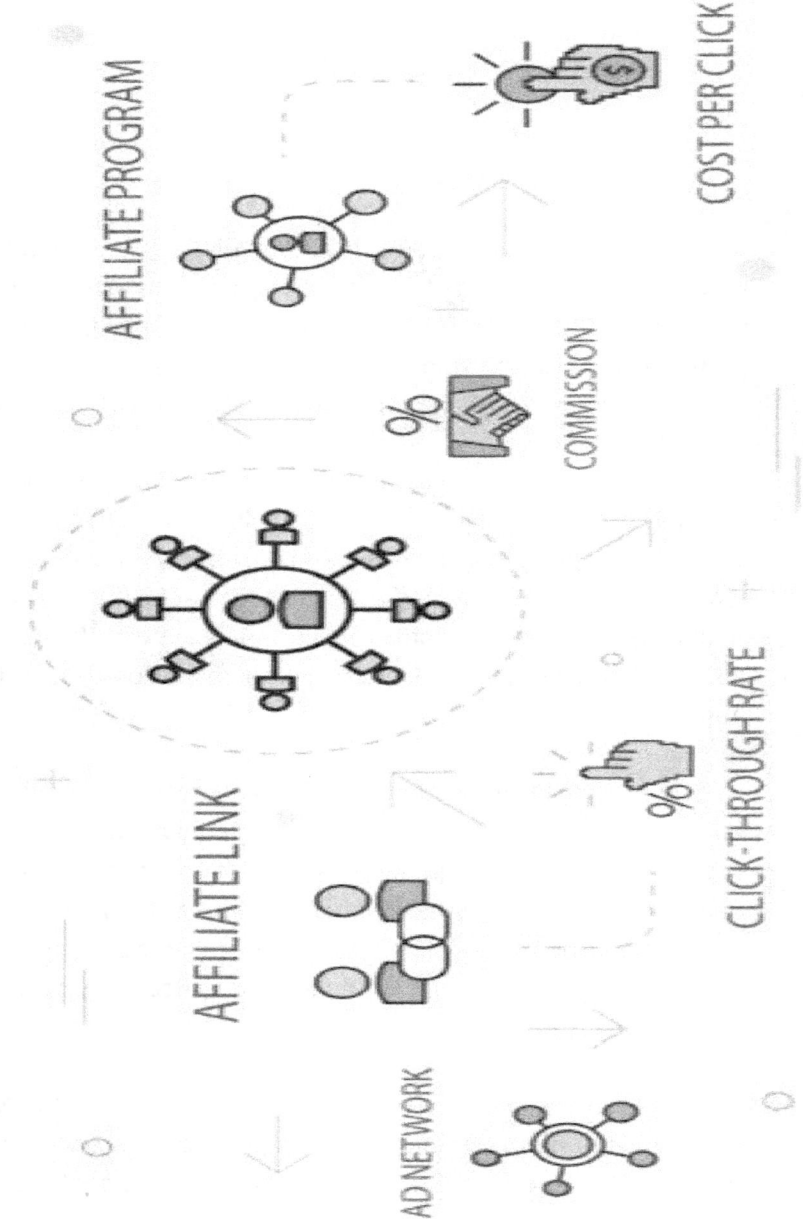

For merchants, affiliate networks provide a convenient way to expand their reach and increase sales without the need for extensive marketing efforts. By partnering with an affiliate network, merchants gain access to a network of pre-screened affiliates who can promote their products or services to a broader audience.

In summary, affiliate networks play a crucial role in the affiliate marketing ecosystem by connecting affiliates and merchants, tracking sales and commissions, and providing valuable support and resources. Whether you're an affiliate looking to monetize your online presence or a merchant seeking to expand your customer base, affiliate networks offer a convenient and effective solution for achieving your goals in the world of affiliate marketing.

3.CHOOSING PROFITABLE NICHES

Selecting the right niche is a critical step in building a successful affiliate marketing business. A niche is a specific segment of the market that appeals to a particular audience with shared interests, needs, or demographics. By focusing on a profitable niche, affiliates can target a more receptive audience, stand out from the competition, and maximize their earning potential.

When choosing a niche, it's essential to consider several factors to ensure its profitability and sustainability. Firstly, assess the demand and competition within the niche. Look for niches with a healthy balance of demand and competition – too much competition may make it challenging to establish a foothold, while too little demand may limit your earning potential. Tools like keyword research and market analysis can help you gauge the demand and competition level within your chosen niche.

Additionally, consider the profitability of the niche. Some niches inherently lend themselves to higher commissions and conversion rates, such as technology, finance, health, and lifestyle. Within these broad categories, there are numerous sub-niches that affiliates can explore, allowing for specialization and differentiation.

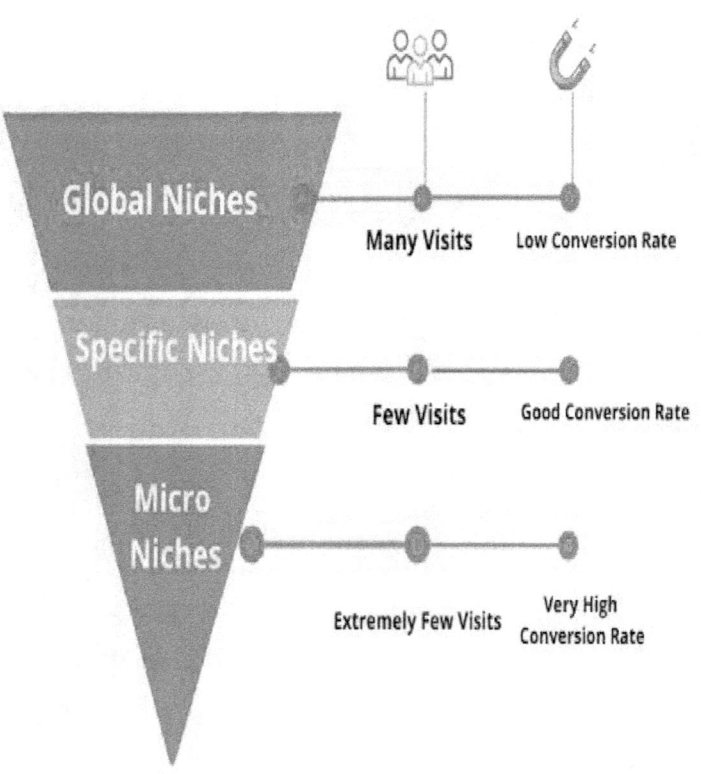

Furthermore, evaluate the audience's willingness to spend within the niche. Niches related to hobbies, passions, or solving specific problems often have highly engaged audiences willing to invest in products or services that enhance their experiences or address their needs.

Lastly, consider your own interests, expertise, and resources when selecting a niche. Choosing a niche that aligns with your passions and knowledge can make the affiliate marketing journey more enjoyable and sustainable in the long run. Additionally, leverage your existing networks, skills, and resources to gain a competitive edge within your chosen niche.

In conclusion, choosing a profitable niche is a foundational step in affiliate marketing success. By carefully assessing demand, competition, profitability, audience willingness to spend, and personal interests, affiliates can identify lucrative niches and position themselves for long-term success in the affiliate marketing industry.

4. SELECTING HIGH CONVERTING PRODUCTS

Choosing the right products to promote is essential for affiliate marketers aiming to maximize their earnings and achieve success in the competitive online landscape. High-converting products not only generate more sales but also result in higher commissions for affiliates. In this guide, we'll explore strategies and considerations for selecting products with the highest conversion rates in affiliate marketing.

• Understand Your Audience: Before selecting products to promote, it's crucial to understand your target audience's needs, preferences, and pain points. Conduct market research, analyze audience demographics, and gather insights into their interests and purchasing behavior. By understanding your audience, you can identify products that resonate with their needs and preferences, increasing the likelihood of conversion.

• Choose Quality Products: Selecting high-quality products is paramount to building trust and credibility with your audience. Choose products from reputable merchants with a track record of delivering quality products and excellent customer service. Consider factors such as product reviews, ratings, and testimonials to gauge the quality and reliability of the products you intend to promote. Promoting subpar products can damage your reputation and credibility as an affiliate marketer, leading to lower conversion rates and diminished long-term success.

- Research Product Demand: Evaluate the demand for the products you plan to promote within your target market. Use keyword research tools, trend analysis, and market research to identify products with high demand and search volume. Look for products that address common pain points or solve specific problems within your niche, as these are more likely to attract potential buyers and result in higher conversion rates.

- Assess Commission Structure: Consider the commission structure offered by merchants for the products you intend to promote. Look for products with competitive commission rates and favorable terms that align with your revenue goals. Some merchants offer tiered commission structures or recurring commissions for subscription-based products, which can result in higher earnings over time. Evaluate the potential earnings per sale and weigh them against the effort required to promote and sell the product.

- Analyze Conversion Metrics: Analyze conversion metrics such as conversion rate, average order value (AOV), and earnings per click (EPC) to assess the performance of potential products. Look for products with high conversion rates and AOV, indicating that they not only convert well but also result in higher earnings per sale. Additionally, consider the EPC, which provides insights into the average earnings generated per click by affiliates promoting the product. High EPC values suggest that affiliates are successfully converting clicks into sales, making the product a potentially lucrative option to promote.

- Consider Seasonality and Trends: Take into account seasonality and trends when selecting products to promote. Certain products experience fluctuations in demand based on seasonal factors, holidays, or trends. Identify evergreen products with consistent

demand year-round, as well as trending products that capitalize on current market trends or consumer preferences. By aligning your product selection with seasonal demand and emerging trends, you can capitalize on opportunities to maximize conversion rates and earnings.

• Diversify Your Product Portfolio: Diversify your product portfolio by promoting a mix of products across different categories or niches. By diversifying your offerings, you can cater to a broader audience and mitigate the risk of relying too heavily on a single product or niche. Consider promoting complementary products or upselling/cross-selling products to increase the value of each sale and maximize your earnings potential.

In conclusion, selecting high-converting products is a strategic process that requires careful consideration of factors such as audience preferences, product quality, demand, commission structure, conversion metrics, seasonality, and trends. By leveraging market insights, conducting thorough research, and diversifying your product portfolio, you can identify and promote products with the highest potential for conversion, ultimately driving revenue and success in affiliate marketing.

5. BUILDING YOUR AFFILIATED WEBSITE

Your affiliate website serves as the cornerstone of your online presence and plays a crucial role in attracting visitors, promoting products, and generating revenue. In this guide, we'll explore the essential steps and considerations for building a successful affiliate website that drives traffic, engages visitors, and converts clicks into sales.

• Choose a Domain Name and Hosting Provider: Start by selecting a domain name that reflects your niche and brand identity. Choose a memorable, descriptive, and SEO-friendly domain name that is easy to spell and pronounce. Once you've chosen a domain name, select a reliable hosting provider that offers fast loading times, reliable uptime, and scalability to accommodate your website's growth.

• Select a Content Management System (CMS): Choose a CMS such as WordPress, Joomla, or Drupal to build and manage your website. WordPress is a popular choice for affiliate marketers due to its ease of use, flexibility, and extensive plugin ecosystem. Select a responsive and customizable theme that aligns with your niche and brand aesthetic, ensuring a seamless user experience across devices.

• Install Essential Plugins: Install and configure essential plugins to enhance the functionality and performance of your affiliate website. Consider plugins for SEO optimization, security, caching, social media integration, and affiliate link management. Plugins such as Yoast SEO, Wordfence Security, and WP Rocket can help optimize your website for search engines, protect against security threats, and improve page load times.

Website					
Ahrefs Link	https://ahrefs.com/site-explorer/ove	https://ahrefs.com/site-explor	https://ahrefs.com/site-explorer/overv	https://ahrefs.com/site-explorer/overv	https://ahrefs.com/site-explorer/o
Key Metrics					
Domain Rating	23	8	9	16	27
Referring Domains	250	105	117	64	163
New Ref. Domains PM (90 days)	37	14	20	15	7
Traffic Analysis					
Monthly Traffic	120,000	119,000	31,000	19,100	4,500
Visit Duration	2:09	0:41	0:21	0:43	0:20
Pages/Session	1.99	1.36	1.17	1.63	1.29
Bounce Rate	60.60%	59.00%	68.00%	46.00%	39.00%
Search Traffic (%)	86%	94%	91%	85%	92%
Social Traffic (%)	0%	0%	0%	0%	0%
Referral Traffic (%)	0%	0%	0%	0%	0%
Direct Traffic (%)	14%	6%	9%	14%	8%
Display Traffic (%)	0%	0%	0%	0%	0%
Email Traffic (%)	0%	0%	0%	0%	0%
Top Referrers					
Referrer 1	-	-	-	-	-
Referrer 2	-	-	-	-	-
Referrer 3	-	-	-	-	-
Countries					
Country 1	38% USA	36% USA	36% USA	17% USA	26% USA
Country 2	12% UK	14% UK	16% UK	12% FRANCE	20% ITALY
Country 3	6% CA	7% FRANCE	5% BULGARIA	11% ITALY	16% GREECE
Content Analysis					
Best By Traffic					
Best By Links					
Best By Shares					
Most FB Likes					
Most Tweets					
Most Pins					
Technical Analysis					
Appealing Design	Basic	Basic	Basic	Buying Guide on Homepage	Buying Guide on Homepage
Anchor Text	Branded/EMD	Branded/Spam	Branded/redirected	Branded/EMD	Branded/EMD
Follow/NoFollow RDs	250 / 153	105/78	117/84	64/17	163/121
Using Sitewides	Few	Few	No	No	No
Shady Links	No	No	No	No	No
Other					

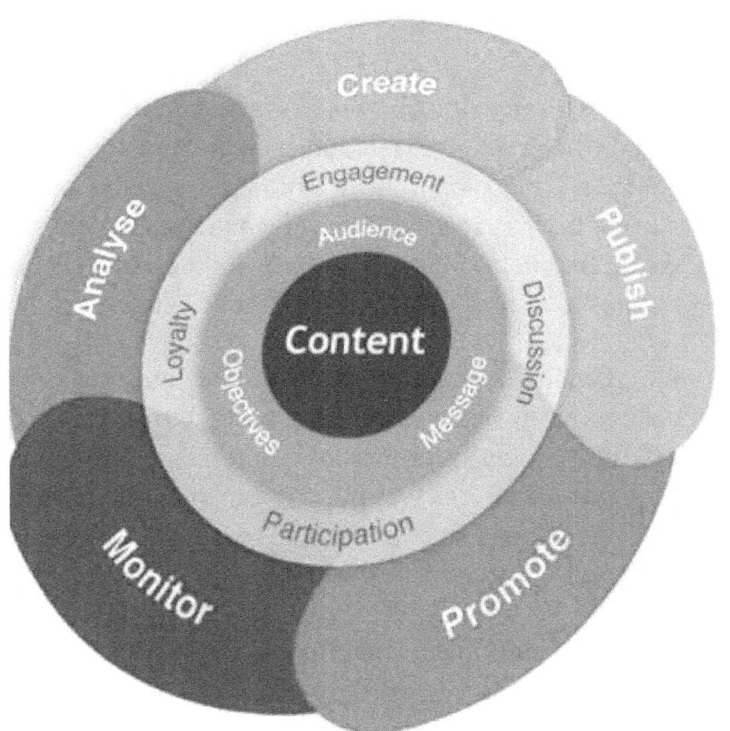

- **Create Compelling Content:** Develop high-quality, engaging content that provides value to your audience and promotes affiliate products effectively. Write informative blog posts, product reviews, tutorials, and guides that address your audience's needs and interests. Incorporate relevant keywords and optimize your content for search engines to attract organic traffic to your website.

- **Implement Affiliate Links and Banners:** Integrate affiliate links and banners strategically within your content to promote products and drive conversions. Use text links, buttons, and banners that blend seamlessly with your website's design and layout. Disclose your affiliate relationships transparently to build trust with your audience and comply with legal requirements.

- **Optimize for Conversions:** Optimize your website for conversions by implementing persuasive call-to-action (CTA) buttons, compelling headlines, and clear product descriptions. Use A/B testing to experiment with different layouts, colors, and messaging to identify the most effective strategies for driving conversions.

- **Monitor and Analyze Performance:** Track and analyze your website's performance using web analytics tools such as Google Analytics. Monitor key metrics such as traffic sources, page views, bounce rate, and conversion rate to identify areas for improvement and optimize your affiliate marketing strategies accordingly.

By following these steps and best practices, you can build a professional, user-friendly affiliate website that attracts visitors, engages them with compelling content, and converts clicks into sales, driving revenue and success in affiliate marketing.

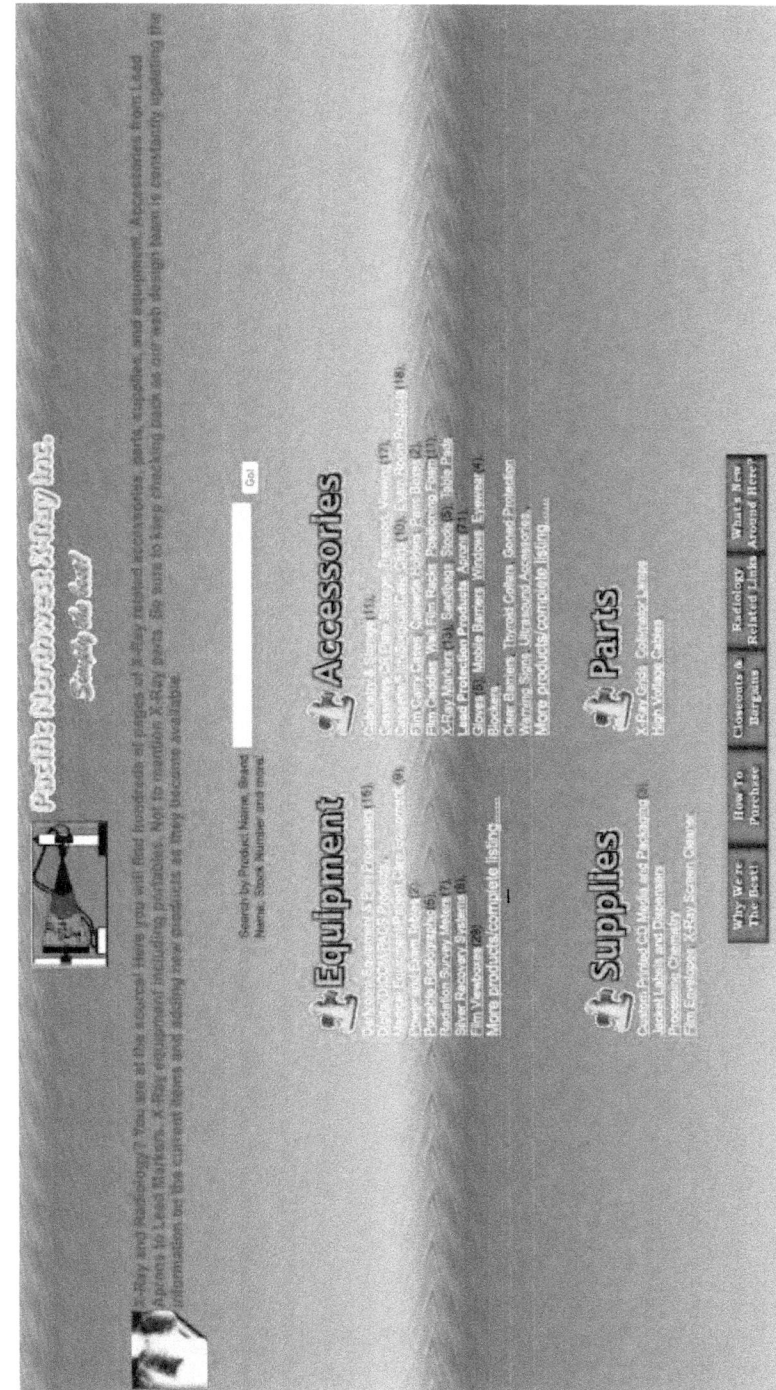

6. CRAFTING COMPELLING CONTENT

Compelling content lies at the heart of successful affiliate marketing efforts. Whether you're writing blog posts, product reviews, tutorials, or social media updates, your content should engage, inform, and persuade your audience to take action. In this guide, we'll explore strategies and best practices for crafting compelling content that drives traffic, builds trust, and converts visitors into customers.

• Know Your Audience: Before creating content, it's essential to understand your target audience's needs, preferences, and pain points. Conduct market research, analyze audience demographics, and gather insights into their interests and challenges. Tailor your content to address their specific needs and provide solutions that resonate with them.

• Provide Value: Focus on providing value to your audience through informative, helpful, and engaging content. Offer practical tips, insights, and advice that help your audience solve problems or achieve their goals. Position yourself as a trusted resource in your niche, and your audience will be more likely to engage with your content and consider your recommendations.

• Be Authentic and Transparent: Authenticity and transparency are crucial for building trust with your audience. Be honest and genuine in your content, sharing your personal experiences, opinions, and insights. Disclose your affiliate relationships openly and transparently, and only promote products that you genuinely believe in and would recommend to others.

• Write Compelling Headlines and Hooks: Capture your audience's attention with compelling headlines and hooks that pique their curiosity and encourage them to read further. Use powerful words and phrases, ask thought-provoking questions, or promise a solution to a problem your audience is facing. Your headline should promise value and create a sense of urgency or excitement to entice readers to click through and engage with your content.

• Use Visuals to Enhance Engagement: Incorporate visuals such as images, infographics, videos, and interactive elements to enhance the appeal and engagement of your content. Visuals help break up text, make your content more visually appealing, and convey information more effectively. Use high-quality, relevant visuals that complement your content and reinforce your message.

• Optimize for SEO: Optimize your content for search engines to attract organic traffic and improve your website's visibility in search results. Conduct keyword research to identify relevant keywords and phrases related to your niche and incorporate them strategically into your content. Use descriptive titles, headings, and meta tags to make your content more discoverable to search engines and users.

• Include Clear Call-to-Actions (CTAs): Guide your audience towards the desired action with clear and compelling call-to-action (CTA) buttons or links. Whether it's to learn more, sign up for a newsletter, or make a purchase, your CTAs should be persuasive, prominently displayed, and easy to click. Use persuasive language and urgency to encourage immediate action from your audience.

By following these strategies and best practices, you can create compelling content that resonates with your audience, drives engagement, and ultimately leads to conversions and success in affiliate marketing. Remember to continuously monitor and analyze the performance of your content, iterate based on feedback and insights, and refine your strategies to achieve optimal results.

Using ChatGPT to generate compelling blog post ideas for affiliate marketing

- A. Niche-specific topics
- B. Trending topics
- C. Problem-solving content

7. EFFECTIVE PROMOTION STRATEGIES

Effective promotion is essential for driving traffic, generating leads, and converting clicks into sales in affiliate marketing. In this guide, we'll explore proven strategies and tactics for promoting affiliate products effectively and maximizing your earning potential.

• Content Marketing: Content marketing involves creating and distributing valuable, relevant, and engaging content to attract and retain your target audience. Write informative blog posts, product reviews, tutorials, and guides that address your audience's needs and interests. Incorporate affiliate links strategically within your content, and focus on providing value and building trust with your audience.

• Email Marketing: Email marketing is a powerful tool for nurturing relationships with your audience and promoting affiliate products. Build an email list of subscribers interested in your niche and send regular newsletters, updates, and promotions. Segment your email list based on interests, preferences, and purchase history to deliver personalized content and offers that resonate with each subscriber.

• Social Media Marketing: Leverage the power of social media to reach and engage your audience on platforms such as Facebook, Instagram, Twitter, LinkedIn, and Pinterest. Create compelling posts, stories, and videos that showcase affiliate products and highlight their benefits. Engage with your followers, respond to comments and messages, and foster a sense of community around your brand.

- Search Engine Optimization (SEO): Optimize your website and content for search engines to improve your visibility and attract organic traffic. Conduct keyword research to identify relevant keywords and phrases related to your niche, and incorporate them strategically into your content, titles, headings, and meta tags. Build high-quality backlinks from reputable websites to improve your website's authority and ranking in search results.

- Paid Advertising: Supplement your organic efforts with paid advertising to reach a broader audience and drive targeted traffic to your affiliate offers. Experiment with various advertising channels such as Google Ads, Facebook Ads, Instagram Ads, and native advertising platforms. Set clear goals, target your ads effectively, and track and analyze your results to optimize your campaigns for maximum ROI.

- Influencer Marketing: Partner with influencers and content creators in your niche to promote affiliate products to their audience. Identify influencers with engaged followers who align with your target market and have credibility and influence in your niche. Collaborate on sponsored content, product reviews, giveaways, and affiliate promotions to leverage their reach and credibility and drive sales.

- Affiliate Contests and Promotions: Encourage engagement and incentivize sales by running affiliate contests, promotions, and bonuses. Offer prizes, incentives, and rewards to top-performing affiliates who drive the most sales or achieve specific milestones. Create urgency and excitement around your promotions to encourage affiliates to promote your offers actively and drive results.

By implementing these effective promotion strategies and experimenting with different tactics, you can increase your visibility, attract qualified traffic, and generate more sales and commissions as an affiliate marketer. Remember to track and analyze your results, iterate based on feedback and insights, and continuously optimize your promotion strategies to achieve optimal results and maximize your earning potential.

8. EMAIL MARKETING FOR AFFILIATES

Email marketing is a powerful tool for affiliate marketers to engage with their audience, nurture relationships, and promote affiliate products effectively. In this guide, we'll explore best practices and strategies for leveraging email marketing to drive conversions and maximize your affiliate earnings.

• Build a Targeted Email List: Start by building an email list of subscribers interested in your niche or industry. Offer valuable incentives such as lead magnets, free guides, or exclusive content to encourage visitors to subscribe to your email list. Segment your email list based on demographics, interests, and purchase behavior to deliver personalized content and offers that resonate with each subscriber.

• Provide Value in Every Email: Focus on providing value to your subscribers in every email you send. Offer helpful tips, insights, and advice related to your niche, and showcase affiliate products that solve specific problems or address your audience's needs. Avoid overly promotional content and prioritize building trust and credibility with your subscribers.

• Craft Compelling Subject Lines: Capture your subscribers' attention and entice them to open your emails with compelling subject lines. Use curiosity, urgency, or personalized language to spark curiosity and encourage opens. Experiment with different subject line strategies and track open rates to identify what resonates most with your audience.

• Incorporate Affiliate Links Strategically: Integrate affiliate links strategically within your email content to promote relevant products and drive conversions. Embed affiliate links within product recommendations, testimonials, or call-to-action buttons that encourage subscribers to click through and make a purchase. Disclose your affiliate relationships transparently to maintain trust with your audience.

• Segment Your Email Campaigns: Segment your email campaigns based on subscriber preferences, interests, and behavior to deliver targeted content and offers. Create separate email sequences for new subscribers, engaged subscribers, and inactive subscribers to tailor your messaging and promotions accordingly. Personalize your emails with dynamic content and recommendations based on each subscriber's profile and past interactions.

• Use Automation and Drip Campaigns: Set up automation and drip campaigns to deliver relevant content and promotions to your subscribers over time. Create welcome sequences to onboard new subscribers and introduce them to your brand and affiliate offerings. Schedule follow-up sequences to nurture leads, re-engage inactive subscribers, and promote affiliate products based on their interests and behavior.

• Monitor and Analyze Performance: Track and analyze key metrics such as open rates, click-through rates, conversion rates, and revenue generated from your email campaigns. Use this data to evaluate the effectiveness of your email marketing efforts, identify areas for improvement, and optimize your campaigns for better results. Test different elements such as subject lines, content, CTAs, and sending times to refine your email strategies and maximize your affiliate earnings.

By implementing these email marketing strategies and best practices, affiliate marketers can effectively engage with their audience, promote affiliate products, and drive conversions through email campaigns. Remember to prioritize providing value to your subscribers, segment your email lists, and continuously monitor and optimize your campaigns to achieve maximum results and maximize your affiliate earnings.

9.HARNESSING THE POWER OF SOCIAL MEDIA

Social media has revolutionized the way affiliate marketers connect with their audience, promote products, and drive conversions. With billions of active users across various platforms, social media offers unparalleled opportunities to reach and engage with your target audience in meaningful ways. Here are some strategies for harnessing the power of social media in affiliate marketing:

• Choose the Right Platforms: Identify the social media platforms where your target audience is most active and engaged. Whether it's Facebook, Instagram, Twitter, LinkedIn, or Pinterest, focus your efforts on platforms where you can reach your audience effectively and build a presence that aligns with your niche and brand.

• Build a Strong Presence: Create a professional and engaging profile on each social media platform, complete with relevant information, branding elements, and a compelling bio. Use high-quality visuals, such as images, videos, and graphics, to grab attention and showcase your affiliate products in an appealing way.

• Provide Value-Driven Content: Focus on providing valuable and relevant content that resonates with your audience's interests, needs, and aspirations. Share informative posts, tips, tutorials, and behind-the-scenes glimpses that add value and establish you as an authority in your niche. Incorporate affiliate links strategically within your content, ensuring they enhance rather than interrupt the user experience.

• Engage and Interact: Foster engagement with your audience by responding to comments, messages, and mentions promptly. Encourage dialogue, ask questions, and spark conversations to deepen connections and build relationships with your followers. Leverage interactive features such as polls, quizzes, and live videos to increase engagement and keep your audience actively involved.

• Promote Affiliate Products: Seamlessly integrate affiliate product promotions into your social media content in a way that feels authentic and genuine. Showcase products through creative storytelling, user-generated content, product reviews, and demonstrations that highlight their benefits and value to your audience. Use persuasive calls-to-action (CTAs) to encourage followers to take action and make purchases.

• Leverage Influencer Partnerships: Collaborate with influencers and content creators in your niche to expand your reach and amplify your affiliate promotions. Partner with influencers who have a relevant and engaged audience that aligns with your target market. Co-create sponsored content, product reviews, giveaways, or affiliate promotions that leverage their influence and credibility to drive sales.

• Analyze Performance and Iterate: Monitor and analyze the performance of your social media efforts using platform analytics and tracking tools. Track key metrics such as engagement rates, click-through rates, conversion rates, and revenue generated from affiliate promotions. Use this data to identify what content resonates with your audience, optimize your strategies, and refine your approach for better results.

By implementing these strategies, affiliate marketers can leverage the power of social media to build brand awareness, engage with their audience, and drive conversions effectively. Remember to

prioritize authenticity, value, and engagement in your social media efforts, and continuously iterate and refine your strategies based on insights and feedback from your audience.

10. SEARCH ENGINE OPTIMIZATION (SEO) FOR AFFILIATES

Search Engine Optimization (SEO) is a crucial component of affiliate marketing success, as it helps affiliates improve their visibility in search engine results and attract organic traffic to their affiliate websites. By optimizing their content and website for search engines, affiliates can increase their chances of ranking higher for relevant keywords, driving more targeted traffic, and ultimately boosting their affiliate earnings. Here are some key strategies for implementing SEO effectively in affiliate marketing:

• Keyword Research: Conduct comprehensive keyword research to identify relevant keywords and phrases that your target audience is searching for. Focus on long-tail keywords with moderate to high search volume and low competition, as they are easier to rank for and tend to attract more qualified traffic. Use keyword research tools such as Google Keyword Planner, SEMrush, or Ahrefs to uncover valuable keyword opportunities.

• On-Page Optimization: Optimize your website's on-page elements, including titles, headings, meta descriptions, and URLs, to make them more search engine-friendly. Incorporate your target keywords naturally within your content while ensuring readability and relevance. Use descriptive and compelling titles and meta descriptions to attract clicks from search engine users and improve your click-through rate (CTR).

• High-Quality Content: Create high-quality, informative, and engaging content that addresses the needs and interests of your target audience. Publish blog posts, articles, product reviews, tutorials, and guides that provide value and solve problems for your audience. Use your target keywords strategically within your content while maintaining a natural and conversational tone.

• Link Building: Build high-quality backlinks from reputable and authoritative websites to improve your website's authority and ranking in search engine results. Focus on acquiring relevant and contextually relevant backlinks from websites within your niche or industry. Guest posting, blogger outreach, and content partnerships are effective strategies for earning backlinks from other websites.

• Mobile Optimization: Ensure that your website is optimized for mobile devices to provide a seamless user experience for mobile users. Use responsive design principles to ensure that your website adapts to different screen sizes and devices. Mobile-friendly websites are favored by search engines and tend to rank higher in mobile search results.

• Page Speed Optimization: Optimize your website's loading speed to improve user experience and search engine rankings. Compress images, minify code, and leverage browser caching to reduce page load times. Use tools like Google PageSpeed Insights or GTmetrix to identify and fix performance issues that may be slowing down your website.

• Monitoring and Analysis: Monitor your website's performance in search engine results using tools like Google Analytics and Google Search Console. Track key metrics such as organic traffic, keyword rankings, and click-through rates to measure the effectiveness of your SEO efforts. Use this data to identify areas for improvement and refine your SEO strategies over time.

By implementing these SEO strategies and best practices, affiliates can increase their visibility in search engine results, attract more targeted traffic, and ultimately improve their affiliate earnings. Remember to focus on providing value to your audience, creating high-quality content, and optimizing your website for both users and search engines to achieve long-term success in affiliate marketing.

11. PAID ADVERTISING TACTICS

Paid advertising is a powerful strategy for affiliate marketers to reach a larger audience, drive targeted traffic, and increase affiliate sales. By investing in paid advertising, affiliates can promote their affiliate products more effectively, generate leads, and maximize their earnings. Here are some effective paid advertising tactics for affiliate marketing:

• Google Ads: Google Ads (formerly known as Google AdWords) is a popular advertising platform that allows affiliates to display ads on Google's search results pages, as well as on websites within the Google Display Network. Affiliates can target specific keywords related to their niche, create compelling ad copy, and bid on relevant keywords to appear at the top of search results and attract clicks from interested users.

• Facebook Ads: Facebook Ads enables affiliates to create targeted advertising campaigns to reach users based on demographics, interests, behaviors, and more. Affiliates can create various types of ads, including image ads, video ads, carousel ads, and lead generation ads, to promote affiliate products to their target audience on Facebook and Instagram.

• Instagram Ads: Instagram Ads allow affiliates to reach a highly engaged audience on one of the most popular social media platforms. Affiliates can create visually appealing ads that blend seamlessly with users' feeds and stories, showcasing affiliate products and driving traffic to their affiliate websites or landing pages.

- Native Advertising: Native advertising involves creating ads that match the form and function of the platform on which they appear, providing a non-disruptive and seamless user experience. Affiliates can leverage native advertising platforms to promote affiliate products through sponsored content, recommended articles, and promoted listings that blend naturally with the surrounding content.

- Influencer Marketing: Influencer marketing involves partnering with social media influencers and content creators to promote affiliate products to their engaged audience. Affiliates can collaborate with influencers in their niche to create sponsored content, product reviews, tutorials, or endorsements that showcase affiliate products and drive conversions through their influence and credibility.

- Retargeting Campaigns: Retargeting campaigns allow affiliates to re-engage users who have previously visited their website or interacted with their content but have not yet made a purchase. Affiliates can use retargeting ads to remind users of products they've viewed, abandoned carts, or special promotions, encouraging them to return to the website and complete the purchase.

- Affiliate Networks: Many affiliate networks offer their own advertising platforms and tools that affiliates can use to promote affiliate products more effectively. Affiliates can access a wide range of advertising options, targeting capabilities, and tracking features through affiliate networks, simplifying the process of running paid advertising campaigns for affiliate products.

By leveraging these paid advertising tactics, affiliates can expand their reach, attract targeted traffic, and increase their affiliate sales and commissions. Remember to set clear goals, target your ads effectively, track and analyze your results, and optimize your campaigns based on performance data to achieve maximum ROI from your paid advertising efforts in affiliate marketing.

12.TRACKING AND ANALYZING PERFORMANCE

Tracking and analyzing performance metrics is essential for affiliate marketers to measure the effectiveness of their marketing efforts, identify areas for improvement, and optimize their strategies for better results. By monitoring key performance indicators (KPIs) and analyzing data, affiliates can make informed decisions, maximize their ROI, and achieve greater success in affiliate marketing. Here's how to effectively track and analyze performance in affiliate marketing:

• Set Clear Goals: Start by defining clear, specific, and measurable goals for your affiliate marketing campaigns. Whether it's increasing website traffic, generating leads, or driving sales, having clear objectives will guide your efforts and provide a benchmark for measuring success.

• Track Affiliate Links and Conversions: Use tracking tools provided by affiliate networks or third-party tracking software to monitor the performance of your affiliate links and track conversions. Track metrics such as clicks, impressions, conversions, and revenue generated from each affiliate link to gauge their effectiveness and identify top-performing products or campaigns.

• Monitor Traffic Sources: Analyze the sources of traffic to your affiliate website or landing pages to understand where your visitors are coming from. Track metrics such as organic search, paid advertising, social media, email marketing, and referral traffic to identify which channels are driving the most traffic and conversions.

• Analyze Conversion Rates: Measure conversion rates for different affiliate products, campaigns, and traffic sources to identify which ones are most effective at converting visitors into customers. Analyze factors that may impact conversion rates, such as website design, user experience, pricing, and promotional strategies, to optimize your conversion funnel for better results.

• Assess Return on Investment (ROI): Calculate the return on investment (ROI) for your affiliate marketing campaigns by comparing the revenue generated from affiliate sales to the costs incurred, including advertising expenses, affiliate commissions, and other marketing costs. Analyze the ROI for individual campaigns or channels to determine their profitability and allocate resources accordingly.

• Utilize Analytics Tools: Use web analytics tools such as Google Analytics, Adobe Analytics, or other tracking platforms to gather data and insights about your website's performance, user behavior, and conversion paths. Set up goals, funnels, and custom reports to track specific actions and metrics that align with your affiliate marketing objectives.

• Test and Iterate: Continuously test different variables, such as ad creatives, landing page designs, messaging, and promotional strategies, to identify what resonates most with your audience and drives the best results. Use A/B testing, split testing, or multivariate testing to experiment with different elements and optimize your campaigns for maximum performance.

• Regularly Review and Optimize: Regularly review your performance data and analytics to identify trends, patterns, and areas for improvement. Use insight from your analysis to refine your strategies, optimize your campaigns, and make data-driven decisions to achieve better results in affiliate marketing.

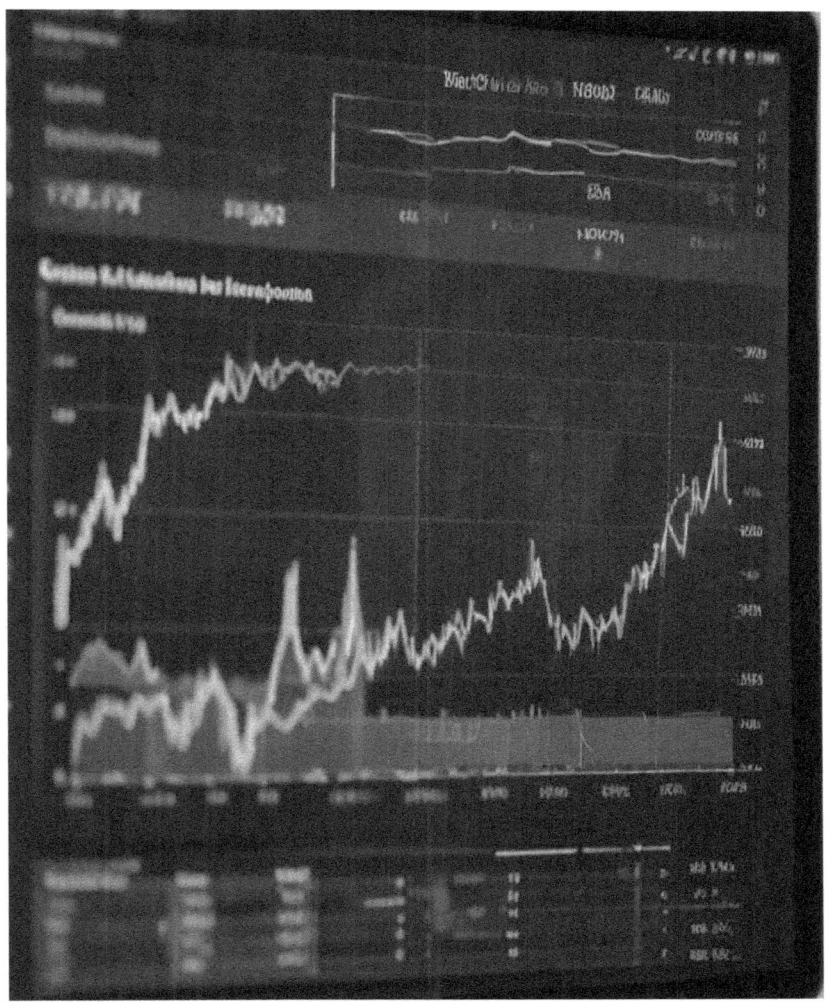

By tracking and analyzing performance metrics effectively, affiliate marketers can gain valuable insights into their campaigns, identify opportunities for growth, and optimize their strategies for maximum impact and success. Remember to set clear goals, utilize analytics tools, test and iterate, and continuously review and optimize your performance to achieve your affiliate marketing objectives.

13. OPTIMIZING CONVERSION RATES

Conversion rate optimization (CRO) is crucial for affiliate marketers looking to maximize their earnings and achieve success in the competitive landscape of affiliate marketing. By optimizing conversion rates, affiliates can increase the percentage of website visitors who take desired actions, such as making a purchase or signing up for a newsletter, ultimately driving more revenue and commissions. Here are some effective strategies for optimizing conversion rates in affiliate marketing:

• Understand Your Audience: Start by understanding your target audience's needs, preferences, and pain points. Conduct market research, analyze audience demographics, and gather insights into their behavior and motivations. Tailor your messaging, offers, and promotions to resonate with your audience and address their specific needs and interests.

• Focus on User Experience (UX): Prioritize creating a seamless and intuitive user experience for your website visitors. Ensure that your website is well-designed, mobile-friendly, and easy to navigate. Optimize page load times, minimize distractions, and streamline the conversion process to reduce friction and make it as easy as possible for users to take action.

• Create Compelling Calls-to-Action (CTAs): Use persuasive and visually appealing calls-to-action (CTAs) to prompt visitors to take the desired action, whether it's making a purchase, signing up for a newsletter, or downloading a resource. Place CTAs strategically throughout your website, and use compelling language and design to grab attention and encourage clicks.

• Test Different Elements: Conduct A/B testing or split testing experiments to test different elements of your website, such as headlines, images, colors, button styles, and page layouts. Experiment with variations to identify what resonates most with your audience and drives the highest conversion rates. Continuously iterate and refine your website based on the results of your tests.

• Offer Incentives and Promotions: Encourage conversions by offering incentives, discounts, or promotions to incentivize visitors to take action. Use limited-time offers, exclusive deals, or freebies to create a sense of urgency and motivate users to act quickly. Highlight the value proposition of your offers and clearly communicate the benefits to entice conversions.

• Provide Social Proof: Leverage social proof to build trust and credibility with your audience and reassure them that they're making the right decision. Incorporate customer testimonials, reviews, ratings, and endorsements to showcase the positive experiences of previous customers and validate the value of your affiliate products or services.

• Optimize Landing Pages: Optimize your landing pages to align with the intent of your traffic and encourage conversions. Ensure that your landing pages are relevant, compelling, and focused on a single objective. Use persuasive copy, persuasive imagery, and clear calls-to-action to guide visitors towards the desired action and minimize distractions that could derail conversions.

• Analyze and Iterate: Continuously monitor and analyze your conversion rates and performance metrics to identify areas for improvement. Use analytics tools to track user behavior, identify bottlenecks in the conversion funnel, and pinpoint opportunities for optimization. Test and iterate on your strategies based on data-driven insights to continuously improve your conversion rates over time.

Conversion Rate Optimization

The process of increasing the percentage of users or website visitors who complete a specific action to increase the number of leads you generate.

By implementing these strategies and best practices, affiliate marketers can optimize their conversion rates, increase their affiliate earnings, and achieve greater success in affiliate marketing. Remember to prioritize user experience, test different elements, offer incentives, and continuously analyze and iterate on your strategies to maximize your conversion rates and drive more revenue from your affiliate campaigns.

14.SCALING YOUR AFFILIATE BUSINESS

Scaling your affiliate business involves expanding your reach, increasing your revenue streams, and optimizing your operations to achieve sustainable growth and long-term success. As you scale your affiliate business, you aim to maximize your earning potential while minimizing your workload and expenses. Here are some effective strategies for scaling your affiliate business:

• Diversify Your Income Streams: Expand your revenue streams beyond affiliate commissions by diversifying your income sources. Explore opportunities such as creating and selling digital products, offering consulting services, hosting webinars or workshops, or monetizing your website through display ads or sponsored content. Diversifying your income streams can help reduce reliance on any single source of revenue and increase your overall earning potential.

• Scale Your Traffic Generation Efforts: Increase your website traffic and audience reach by scaling your traffic generation efforts. Invest in content marketing, search engine optimization (SEO), paid advertising, social media marketing, email marketing, and other strategies to attract more visitors to your website or affiliate offers. Continuously optimize your traffic generation strategies to reach new audiences and expand your reach.

• Expand Your Product Portfolio: Expand your affiliate product portfolio by partnering with additional merchants or affiliate networks

and promoting a wider range of products and services within your niche. Identify complementary products or related niches that align with your audience's interests and needs. By diversifying your product offerings, you can cater to a broader audience and increase your earning potential.

• Automate and Outsource Tasks: Automate repetitive tasks and outsource non-core activities to free up your time and focus on high-value tasks that drive growth. Use tools and software to automate email marketing, social media scheduling, content distribution, and other routine tasks. Hire freelancers or virtual assistants to handle administrative tasks, content creation, graphic design, or customer support, allowing you to scale more efficiently.

• Invest in Scalable Systems and Infrastructure: Invest in scalable systems, processes, and infrastructure to support your growing affiliate business. Upgrade your website hosting, implement robust analytics and tracking systems, and invest in customer relationship management (CRM) software or affiliate management platforms to streamline your operations and handle increased traffic and sales volume effectively.

• Build Strategic Partnerships: Collaborate with other affiliate marketers, influencers, bloggers, or industry experts to leverage their audience and expand your reach. Partner with complementary businesses or brands for co-promotions, joint ventures, or affiliate partnerships. Building strategic partnerships can help you tap into new markets, gain access to new audiences, and grow your affiliate business more rapidly.

• Focus on Value and Customer Experience: Prioritize providing value and delivering an exceptional customer experience to your audience. Create high-quality content, offer valuable insights and resources, and provide excellent customer support to build trust and loyalty with your audience. By focusing on delivering value and meeting the needs of your audience, you can attract repeat customers, generate referrals, and sustain long-term growth.

• Track and Measure Key Metrics: Continuously track and measure key performance metrics such as revenue, traffic, conversion rates, average order value (AOV), customer lifetime value (CLV), and return on investment (ROI). Use analytics tools and reporting dashboards to gain insights into your affiliate business's performance and identify areas for improvement. Adjust your strategies based on data-driven insights to optimize your growth and maximize your profitability.

By implementing these strategies and best practices, you can scale your affiliate business effectively, increase your revenue, and achieve sustainable growth over time. Remember to focus on providing value, diversifying your income streams, automating processes, and continuously optimizing your strategies to scale your affiliate business successfully.

15. MONETIZATION BEYOND AFFILIATE MARKETING

While affiliate marketing is a popular and effective way to monetize your online presence, there are numerous other opportunities to diversify your income streams and maximize your earning potential. Here are some alternative monetization methods to consider:

• Digital Products: Create and sell digital products such as e-books, online courses, templates, guides, or software tools related to your niche. Digital products offer high profit margins and can be sold repeatedly without the need for inventory or shipping.

• Membership Sites: Launch a membership site or subscription-based service offering exclusive content, resources, community access, or premium features to members. Charge a monthly or annual fee for access to your membership site and provide ongoing value to your subscribers.

• Sponsored Content: Partner with brands or advertisers to create sponsored content, sponsored posts, sponsored videos, or sponsored social media posts. Charge a fee for featuring sponsored content on your website, blog, social media channels, or email newsletters.

• Advertising: Monetize your website or blog through display advertising, such as Google AdSense, Media.net, or other ad networks. Display ads on your website and earn revenue based on ad impressions or clicks. Consider optimizing your ad placements and ad formats to maximize your ad revenue.

• Freelancing or Consulting: Offer freelance services or consulting expertise in your niche, such as writing, design, marketing, SEO, social media management, or coaching. Leverage your skills and expertise to provide value to clients and charge fees for your services on a project basis or hourly rate.

• Sponsorships and Partnerships: Secure sponsorships or brand partnerships with companies, brands, or influencers within your niche. Collaborate on sponsored content, co-branded campaigns, affiliate partnerships, or event sponsorships in exchange for monetary compensation or other benefits.

• Online Events or Workshops: Host online events, webinars, workshops, or virtual summits on topics relevant to your audience's interests. Charge admission fees or offer premium access to exclusive content, speakers, or networking opportunities.

• Physical Products: Develop and sell physical products such as merchandise, branded merchandise, or merchandise related to your niche. Use print-on-demand services, dropshipping, or fulfillment partners to handle inventory, production, and shipping logistics.

• Licensing and Syndication: License your content, images, videos, or intellectual property to third-party publishers, media outlets, or content platforms. Earn royalties or licensing fees for the use of your content in other media channels or publications.

• Donations or Crowdfunding: Accept donations or crowdfunding contributions from your audience through platforms such as Patreon, Ko-fi, or PayPal. Offer exclusive perks, rewards, or incentives to supporters in exchange for their financial contributions.

Understanding and Optimizing Website Monetization Strategies

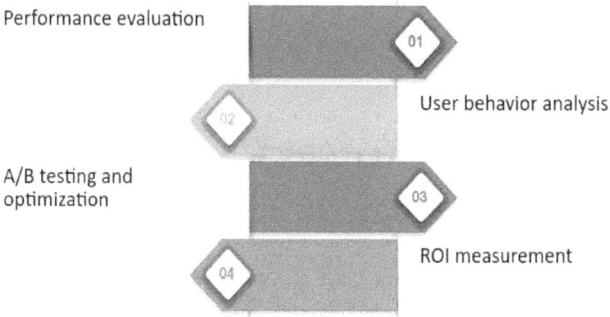

By exploring these alternative monetization methods, you can diversify your income streams, reduce reliance on any single source of revenue, and maximize your earning potential as a content creator, influencer, or online entrepreneur. Evaluate your audience's preferences, interests, and purchasing behavior to determine which monetization strategies align best with your brand and business goals.

16. LEGAL AND ETHICAL CONSIDERATIONS

As an affiliate marketer, it's crucial to adhere to legal and ethical guidelines to maintain trust with your audience, comply with regulations, and protect your reputation. Here are some key legal and ethical considerations to keep in mind:

• Disclosure of Affiliate Relationships: Transparency is essential in affiliate marketing. Disclose your affiliate relationships clearly and conspicuously to your audience whenever you promote affiliate products or services. Use clear language such as "This post contains affiliate links" or "I may earn a commission for purchases made through these links" to inform your audience about your financial interests.

• Compliance with Regulations: Familiarize yourself with relevant laws and regulations governing affiliate marketing, such as the Federal Trade Commission (FTC) guidelines in the United States. Ensure that your promotional content complies with advertising laws, consumer protection regulations, and disclosure requirements. Stay updated on any changes or updates to regulations that may affect your affiliate marketing practices.

• Truthfulness and Accuracy: Ensure that your promotional content is truthful, accurate, and not misleading to your audience. Avoid making exaggerated claims, false promises, or deceptive statements about affiliate products or services. Provide honest and unbiased reviews, recommendations, and endorsements based on your genuine experiences and opinions.

• Respect for Intellectual Property: Respect copyright laws and intellectual property rights when creating content for affiliate marketing purposes. Obtain proper permissions or licenses for any third-party content, images, or materials used in your promotions. Avoid infringing on trademarks, copyrights, or other intellectual property rights of others.

• Privacy and Data Protection: Protect the privacy and data of your audience in accordance with applicable privacy laws and regulations. Obtain consent before collecting personal information from visitors or subscribers, and clearly disclose how their data will be used, stored, and shared. Implement appropriate security measures to safeguard sensitive information and prevent unauthorized access or data breaches.

• Avoiding Unethical Practices: Avoid engaging in unethical practices such as spamming, blackhat SEO techniques, deceptive advertising, or manipulative tactics to boost your affiliate commissions. Build trust with your audience by providing value, delivering quality content, and acting with integrity in all your affiliate marketing activities.

• Compliance with Affiliate Network Policies: Adhere to the terms and conditions of affiliate programs and networks you participate in. Familiarize yourself with their policies, guidelines, and prohibited practices to ensure compliance with their rules. Violating affiliate network policies could result in account suspension, termination, or loss of commissions.

Legal Considerations for Affiliate Marketing

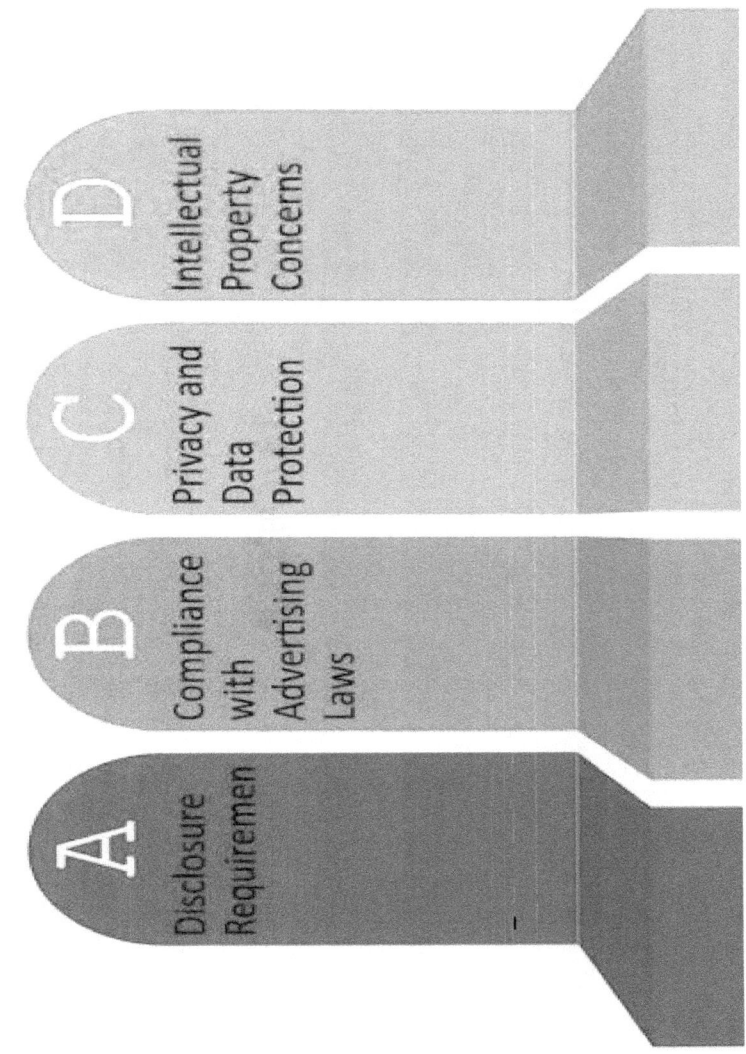

- **A** — Disclosure Requiremen
- **B** — Compliance with Advertising Laws
- **C** — Privacy and Data Protection
- **D** — Intellectual Property Concerns

- **Full Disclosure of Material Connections:** Disclose any material connections, affiliations, or incentives you have with brands, merchants, or products you promote as an affiliate. Be transparent about any compensation, free products, discounts, or other benefits you receive in exchange for promoting affiliate products to your audience.

By following these legal and ethical considerations, you can build a trustworthy reputation, maintain compliance with regulations, and foster positive relationships with your audience as an affiliate marketer. Prioritize honesty, transparency, and integrity in all your affiliate marketing activities to establish credibility and earn the trust of your audience over the long term.

17. OVERCOMING COMMON CHALLENGES

While affiliate marketing offers tremendous opportunities for earning passive income and building a successful online business, it also comes with its own set of challenges. Here are some common challenges faced by affiliate marketers and strategies for overcoming them:

• Finding Profitable Niches: Challenge: Identifying profitable niches with sufficient demand and low competition can be challenging, especially for new affiliate marketers. Solution: Conduct thorough market research to identify niche markets with high demand, low competition, and profit potential. Explore niche-specific forums, communities, keyword research tools, and affiliate networks to uncover profitable opportunities. Focus on niches that align with your interests, expertise, and audience preferences.

• Generating Quality Traffic: Challenge: Attracting high-quality traffic to your affiliate website or offers can be difficult, especially without a solid traffic generation strategy. Solution: Implement a comprehensive traffic generation strategy that combines organic and paid traffic sources. Utilize search engine optimization (SEO), content marketing, social media marketing, email marketing, influencer partnerships, and paid advertising to attract targeted traffic to your affiliate offers. Focus on providing value, solving problems, and addressing the needs of your audience to attract engaged visitors.

• Building Trust and Credibility: Challenge: Establishing trust and credibility with your audience is essential for successful affiliate marketing, but it can take time and effort to build. Solution: Focus on building authentic relationships with your audience by providing valuable content, demonstrating expertise, and delivering on your promises. Be transparent, honest, and ethical in your marketing efforts, and disclose your affiliate relationships openly. Prioritize building trust and credibility over short-term gains, and consistently deliver value to your audience to earn their trust over time.

• Converting Visitors into Customers: Challenge: Converting website visitors into paying customers can be a significant challenge, especially if your conversion funnel is not optimized. Solution: Optimize your conversion funnel by improving your website design, user experience, and call-to-action (CTA) strategies. Create compelling content, persuasive CTAs, and irresistible offers to encourage visitors to take action. Use A/B testing, split testing, and analytics to identify areas for improvement and optimize your conversion rates continuously.

• Managing Affiliate Relationships: Challenge: Managing relationships with multiple affiliate programs, merchants, and networks can become overwhelming, especially as your affiliate business grows. Solution: Streamline your affiliate relationships by consolidating your partnerships, focusing on high-performing programs, and prioritizing quality over quantity. Use affiliate management platforms, tracking software, and analytics tools to monitor your affiliate activities, track performance metrics, and manage commissions effectively. Communicate regularly with your affiliate partners, and negotiate mutually beneficial terms and agreements.

• Staying Motivated and Persistent: Challenge: Maintaining motivation and persistence in the face of setbacks, challenges, and slow progress can be difficult, especially for new affiliate marketers. Solution: Stay focused on your goals, maintain a positive mindset, and celebrate small victories along the way. Set realistic expectations, and understand that success in affiliate marketing takes time, effort, and perseverance. Surround yourself with a supportive community of fellow affiliate marketers, mentors, and peers who can provide encouragement, guidance, and accountability.

By proactively addressing these common challenges and implementing effective strategies to overcome them, you can increase your chances of success and achieve your goals as an affiliate marketer. Remember to stay adaptable, continuously learn and improve, and embrace challenges as opportunities for growth and development in your affiliate marketing journey.

18. FUTURE TRENDS IN AFFILIATED MARKETING

As technology evolves and consumer behaviors shift, the landscape of affiliate marketing continues to evolve. Here are some future trends shaping the future of affiliate marketing:

• Influencer Affiliate Marketing: Influencer marketing is expected to play an even bigger role in affiliate marketing as influencers become key partners for brands and merchants. Influencers have the ability to reach niche audiences and drive targeted traffic to affiliate offers, making them valuable partners for affiliate marketers.

• AI and Machine Learning: Artificial intelligence (AI) and machine learning technologies are revolutionizing affiliate marketing by enabling marketers to analyze data, predict consumer behavior, and optimize their campaigns more effectively. AI-powered tools can automate tasks such as content creation, audience targeting, and campaign optimization, leading to greater efficiency and improved results.

• Personalization and Customization: Personalization will become increasingly important in affiliate marketing as marketers seek to deliver more relevant and personalized experiences to their audience. By leveraging data and technology, affiliate marketers can segment their audience, tailor their messaging, and recommend products based on individual preferences and behavior.

• Voice Search Optimization: With the rise of voice-enabled devices and virtual assistants, voice search optimization will become essential for affiliate marketers. Optimizing content and websites for voice search queries will help affiliates capture organic traffic and stay ahead of the curve in an increasingly voice-driven search landscape.

• Video Content and Live Streaming: Video content and live streaming are becoming dominant forms of content consumption, presenting new opportunities for affiliate marketers to engage with their audience. Affiliates can create video reviews, tutorials, product demonstrations, and live streams to showcase affiliate products and drive conversions through visual storytelling.

• Niche and Micro-Influencers: As competition increases in mainstream affiliate niches, affiliates will increasingly focus on niche and micro-influencer partnerships to reach more targeted audiences. Niche influencers have smaller but highly engaged audiences, making them valuable partners for affiliates looking to connect with specific demographics or interest groups.

• Affiliate Subscription Models: Subscription-based affiliate models are expected to gain traction, allowing affiliates to earn recurring commissions for ongoing subscriptions or memberships. Affiliates can promote subscription services, software-as-a-service (SaaS) products, online courses, or membership sites that offer recurring revenue opportunities.

• Cross-Channel Marketing: Cross-channel marketing strategies that integrate multiple channels and touchpoints will become more prevalent in affiliate marketing. By leveraging a combination of channels such as social media, email marketing, content marketing, and paid advertising, affiliates can create cohesive, omnichannel experiences that drive engagement and conversions.

• Blockchain and Cryptocurrency: Blockchain technology and cryptocurrency payments are poised to disrupt traditional affiliate marketing models by providing more secure, transparent, and

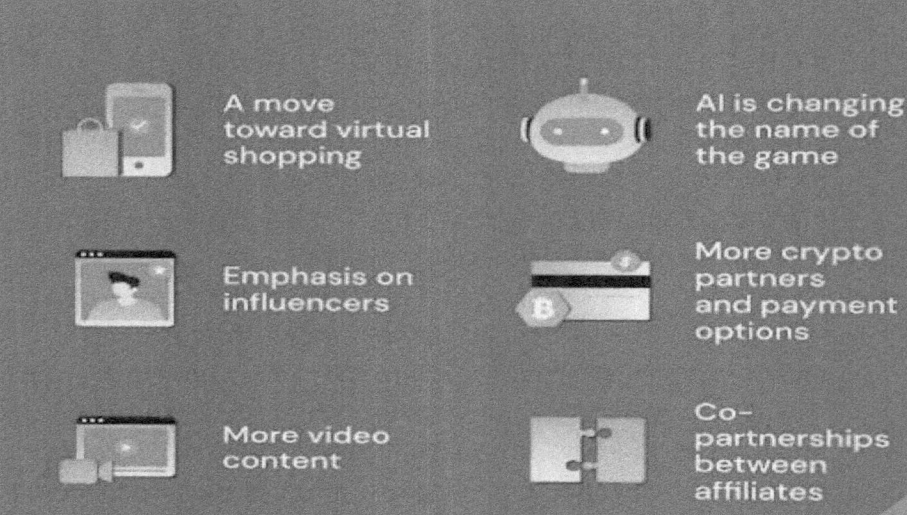

efficient transaction processes. Blockchain-based affiliate networks and smart contracts can help streamline payments, reduce fraud, and increase trust between affiliates and merchants.

• Sustainability and Ethical Marketing: As consumers become more conscious of sustainability and ethical practices, affiliate marketers will need to align with values-driven brands and promote products that prioritize sustainability, social responsibility, and ethical sourcing. Affiliates can capitalize on the growing demand for eco-friendly, fair trade, and socially responsible products and services.

By embracing these future trends and adapting to the changing landscape of affiliate marketing, marketers can stay ahead of the curve, drive innovation, and capitalize on new opportunities for growth and success in the evolving affiliate marketing industry.

19. SUCCESS STORIES AND CASE STUDIES

• **Health and Wellness Blog Monetization:** Sarah, a health and wellness enthusiast, started a blog to share her journey to a healthier lifestyle. Through consistent content creation and strategic affiliate partnerships with health and fitness brands, Sarah was able to monetize her blog effectively. By recommending products she genuinely believed in and providing valuable insights and resources to her audience, Sarah grew her affiliate income steadily over time. Today, Sarah's blog generates passive income through affiliate commissions, sponsorships, and digital product sales, allowing her to pursue her passion full-time.

• **Tech Review YouTube Channel Growth:** John, a tech enthusiast, launched a YouTube channel to share reviews, tutorials, and tips on the latest gadgets and technology trends. By leveraging affiliate marketing partnerships with e-commerce platforms and tech brands, John monetized his channel and earned commissions for recommending products featured in his videos. With a focus on providing honest and unbiased reviews, John gained the trust of his audience and grew his subscriber base rapidly. Today, John's YouTube channel is a thriving affiliate marketing business, generating significant revenue through affiliate commissions and sponsored content partnerships.

• **Fashion Influencer Instagram Success:** Emily, a fashion influencer with a large following on Instagram, partnered with fashion brands and e-commerce retailers to monetize her social media presence through affiliate marketing. By showcasing trendy outfits, styling tips, and fashion hauls featuring affiliate products, Emily was able to drive traffic and sales for her affiliate partners. With a keen eye for aesthetics and a knack for engaging storytelling, Emily's Instagram feed became a go-to destination for fashion inspiration, earning her substantial affiliate commissions and brand collaborations.

• **Travel Blog Passive Income:** Mark, an avid traveler and blogger, turned his passion for travel into a profitable affiliate marketing business. By sharing travel guides, destination reviews, and travel tips on his blog, Mark attracted a loyal audience of fellow travel enthusiasts. Through strategic affiliate partnerships with travel booking platforms, airlines, and travel gear brands, Mark monetized his blog and earned commissions for bookings and product referrals. With a combination of compelling content, SEO optimization, and affiliate partnerships, Mark's travel blog generates passive income while he explores the world.

• **Parenting Website Affiliate Revenue:** Lisa, a parenting blogger and mother of two, created a website to share parenting advice, tips, and resources for fellow parents. Through affiliate marketing partnerships with baby product retailers, parenting book publishers, and educational toy brands, Lisa monetized her website and earned commissions for product recommendations and referrals. By providing valuable content that resonated with her target audience and addressing common parenting challenges, Lisa's website became a trusted resource for parents, generating consistent affiliate revenue and sponsorship opportunities.

These success stories and case studies illustrate the diverse opportunities for monetization and growth in affiliate marketing. By leveraging their expertise, passion, and creativity, these affiliate marketers were able to build profitable businesses and achieve success in their respective niches.

20. CONCLUSION AND NEXT STEPS

In conclusion, affiliate marketing offers a dynamic and lucrative opportunity for individuals and businesses to monetize their online presence, drive revenue, and build successful businesses. Through strategic partnerships, valuable content creation, and audience engagement, affiliate marketers can leverage their influence to promote products and services to their audience while earning commissions for successful referrals. As we've explored, the future of affiliate marketing is filled with exciting trends and opportunities, including influencer marketing, AI and machine learning, personalization, and more.

As you continue your journey in affiliate marketing, here are some next steps to consider:

• **Continuous Learning and Education:** Stay informed about the latest trends, best practices, and strategies in affiliate marketing by investing in continuous learning and education. Attend industry conferences, workshops, webinars, and online courses to expand your knowledge and skills.

• **Diversification of Income Streams:** Explore opportunities to diversify your income streams beyond affiliate marketing by monetizing your expertise through digital products, memberships, sponsored content, consulting, or other revenue streams.

• **Networking and Collaboration:** Build relationships with fellow affiliate marketers, influencers, brands, and industry experts through networking, collaboration, and partnerships. Leverage your network to exchange ideas, share insights, and collaborate on projects to mutual benefit.

- **Data Analysis and Optimization:** Continuously analyze your performance data, track key metrics, and optimize your affiliate marketing campaigns based on data-driven insights. Experiment with different strategies, test new approaches, and iterate on your tactics to maximize your results.

- **Ethical and Transparent Practices:** Prioritize ethical and transparent practices in your affiliate marketing efforts by providing value, disclosing affiliate relationships, and adhering to legal and regulatory requirements. Build trust and credibility with your audience by acting with integrity and authenticity in all your interactions.

- **Adaptation to Industry Changes:** Stay adaptable and flexible in response to changes in the affiliate marketing landscape, including shifts in consumer behavior, technological advancements, and regulatory updates. Embrace innovation, experiment with new platforms and technologies, and pivot your strategies as needed to stay ahead of the curve.

- **Persistence and Resilience:** Success in affiliate marketing often requires persistence, resilience, and a long-term mindset. Stay committed to your goals, persevere through challenges and setbacks, and celebrate your progress and achievements along the way.

By following these next steps and embracing the opportunities and challenges of affiliate marketing, you can continue to grow and thrive in this dynamic and rewarding industry. Whether you're a seasoned affiliate marketer or just starting out, the possibilities for success are endless in the ever-evolving world of affiliate marketing.

21. RESOURCES AND TOOLS

Affiliate marketing requires a combination of strategy, creativity, and technology to succeed in driving traffic, conversions, and revenue. Here are some essential resources and tools that can help affiliate marketers streamline their workflows, optimize their campaigns, and achieve better results:

• **Affiliate Networks:** Joining reputable affiliate networks such as Amazon Associates, ShareASale, CJ Affiliate, Rakuten Advertising, or ClickBank provides access to a wide range of affiliate programs and merchants across various niches. These platforms offer tracking, reporting, and payment processing services, making it easier for affiliates to manage multiple partnerships in one place.

• **Affiliate Tracking Software:** Affiliate tracking software such as Voluum, TUNE, Post Affiliate Pro, or AffTrack allows affiliates to track clicks, conversions, and commissions accurately. These tools provide insights into campaign performance, traffic sources, and audience behavior, enabling affiliates to optimize their campaigns and maximize their ROI.

• **Keyword Research Tools:** Keyword research tools such as SEMrush, Ahrefs, Moz, or Google Keyword Planner help affiliates identify high-volume keywords, analyze competition, and discover content opportunities. By conducting keyword research, affiliates can optimize their content for search engines, attract organic traffic, and target lucrative keywords relevant to their niche.

• **Content Creation Tools:** Content creation tools such as Canva, Adobe Creative Cloud, or Grammarly assist affiliates in creating high-quality content, graphics, and written copy for their websites, blogs, social media, and email marketing campaigns. These tools help affiliates produce engaging, visually appealing content that resonates with their audience and drives conversions.

• **Email Marketing Platforms:** Email marketing platforms such as Mailchimp, ConvertKit, AWeber, or GetResponse enable affiliates to build and nurture email lists, automate email campaigns, and communicate with subscribers effectively. Email marketing is a powerful tool for affiliate marketers to promote products, share valuable content, and drive affiliate sales through targeted email campaigns.

• **Analytics and Reporting Tools:** Analytics and reporting tools such as Google Analytics, Adobe Analytics, or Hotjar provide insights into website traffic, user behavior, and conversion metrics. By analyzing data and performance metrics, affiliates can track the effectiveness of their marketing efforts, identify areas for improvement, and make data-driven decisions to optimize their campaigns.

• **Social Media Management Tools:** Social media management tools such as Buffer, Hootsuite, or Sprout Social help affiliates schedule posts, monitor social media engagement, and analyze social media performance. These tools streamline social media marketing efforts, allowing affiliates to grow their presence, engage with their audience, and promote affiliate products across various social platforms.

By leveraging these resources and tools effectively, affiliate marketers can enhance their productivity, streamline their processes, and achieve better results in their affiliate marketing efforts. Whether it's tracking conversions, optimizing content, or engaging with their audience, having the right tools at their disposal can make a significant difference in the success of affiliate marketing campaigns.

- 74

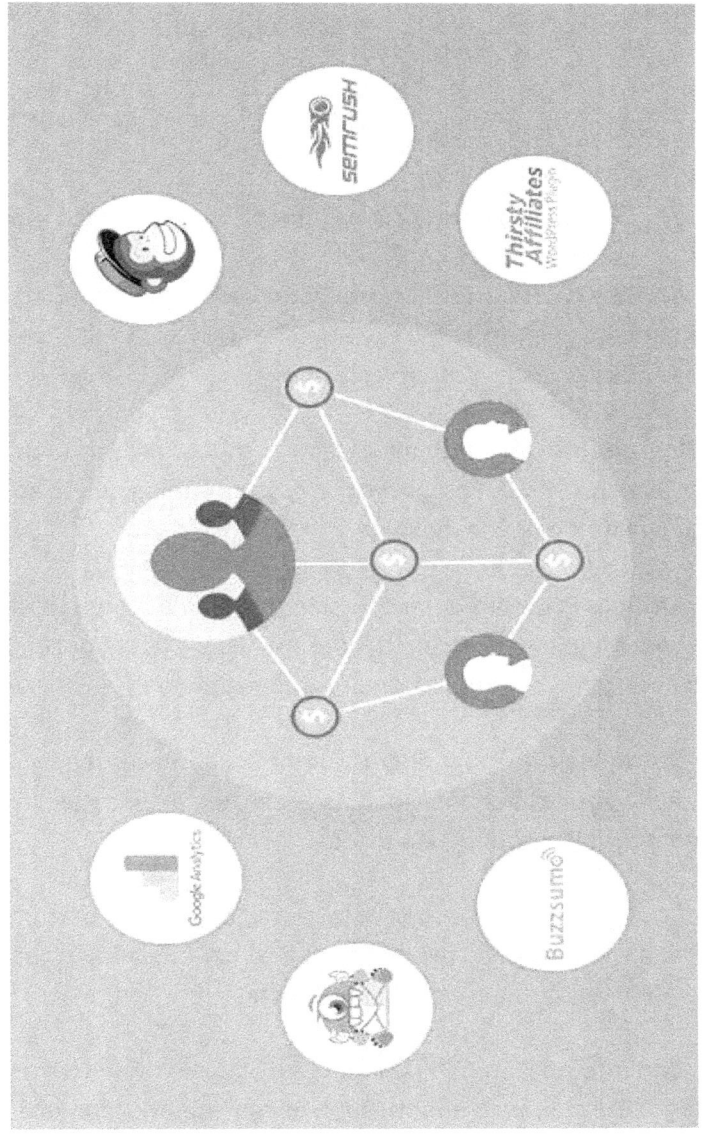

22.GLOSSARY OF AFFILIATE MARKETING TERMS

• **Affiliate:** An individual or entity that promotes products or services offered by another company (merchant) in exchange for a commission for successful referrals or sales.

• **Merchant:** The company or retailer that offers products or services through an affiliate program and pays commissions to affiliates for driving traffic, leads, or sales.

• **Affiliate Program:** A partnership between a merchant and affiliates where affiliates promote the merchant's products or services in exchange for a commission on successful referrals or sales.

• **Commission:** The monetary compensation earned by affiliates for driving desired actions, such as clicks, leads, or sales, for the merchant's products or services.

• **Cookie:** A small piece of data stored on a user's device when they visit a website, used to track their interactions and attribute referrals to affiliates within a certain timeframe.

• **Conversion Rate:** The percentage of website visitors or leads that complete a desired action, such as making a purchase or signing up, as a result of clicking on an affiliate link or advertisement.

• **EPC (Earnings Per Click):** A metric used to measure the average earnings generated by each click on an affiliate link, calculated by dividing total earnings by the number of clicks.

• **ROI (Return on Investment):** The ratio of net profit to the cost of investment, used to measure the profitability of affiliate marketing campaigns and advertising efforts.

• **Niche:** A specific segment or category within a larger market, often targeted by affiliates to focus their marketing efforts and attract a more targeted audience.

• **Conversion Tracking:** The process of tracking and recording the actions taken by users after clicking on an affiliate link, typically using tracking pixels, cookies, or unique affiliate codes.

• **Payment Threshold:** The minimum amount of earnings that affiliates must accumulate before they can request a payout or receive payment from the affiliate program.

• **Subaffiliate:** An affiliate who is recruited by another affiliate (the primary affiliate) to join the affiliate program and promote the merchant's products or services, earning commissions for successful referrals.

• **Cookie Duration:** The length of time that a cookie remains valid on a user's device after clicking on an affiliate link, during which the affiliate can receive credit for subsequent purchases or actions made by the user.

• **Creative:** The promotional materials provided by merchants to affiliates, including banners, text links, product images, and other marketing assets used to promote affiliate products or services.

- **Affiliate Network:** A platform or intermediary that connects merchants with affiliates, facilitates tracking and reporting of affiliate activities, and manages payments and commissions for affiliate marketing campaigns.

Understanding these affiliate marketing terms is essential for navigating the affiliate marketing industry, communicating effectively with affiliate partners, and maximizing your success as an affiliate marketer.

23. INDEX

- Introduction to Affiliate Marketing
- Definition and Basics
- Evolution and Growth of Affiliate Marketing
- Benefits and Opportunities of Affiliate Marketing
- Overview of Affiliate Marketing Ecosystem
- Getting Started in Affiliate Marketing
- Setting Goals and Objectives
- Choosing a Profitable Niche
- Researching and Selecting Affiliate Programs
- Creating a Strategic Affiliate Marketing Plan
- Building Your Affiliate Marketing Strategy
- Understanding Your Audience
- Developing Content and Marketing Channels
- Crafting Compelling Offers and Promotions

- Leveraging Affiliate Marketing Tools and Resources
- Creating Content for Affiliate Marketing
- Content Creation Best Practices
- Writing Product Reviews and Recommendations
- Creating Tutorials, Guides, and How-To Content
- Optimizing Content for Search Engines and Social Media
- Driving Traffic and Conversions
- Traffic Generation Strategies
- Search Engine Optimization (SEO) for Affiliates
- Social Media Marketing and Influencer Partnerships
- Email Marketing and List Building Techniques
- Maximizing Affiliate Revenue
- Conversion Optimization Tactics
- Tracking and Analyzing Affiliate Performance
- Scaling Your Affiliate Business
- Monetization Beyond Affiliate Marketing
- Legal and Ethical Considerations
- Disclosure and Compliance Requirements

- Protecting Consumer Privacy and Data

- Ethical Marketing Practices

- Handling Disputes and Resolving Issues

- Future Trends and Innovations

- Emerging Technologies in Affiliate Marketing

- Predictions and Insights for the Future of Affiliate Marketing

- Adapting to Industry Changes and Evolving Trends

- Case Studies and Success Stories

- Real-Life Examples of Successful Affiliate Marketing Campaigns

- Lessons Learned and Best Practices from Affiliate Marketing Experts

- Inspirational Stories of Affiliate Marketing Success

- Resources and Tools for Affiliate Marketers

- Essential Tools and Software for Affiliate Marketing

- Recommended Books, Blogs, and Resources

- Affiliate Networks and Platforms

- Training Programs and Educational Resources

- Conclusion and Next Steps

- Summary of Key Takeaways

- Actionable Step

NOTES:

www.ingramcontent.com/pod-product-compliance
Lightning Source LLC
Chambersburg PA
CBHW070352230526
45471CB00006B/2535